ZELLA MCFINNLEY

Mommin' Ain't Easy

Simple guidance for difficult days. Six lessons and mantras for first time moms.

*This book was professionally typeset on Reedsy.
Find out more at reedsy.com*

To all of the mothers that appear fearless even when they are scared, who smile even on their hardest of days, who love their children endlessly and live life selflessly.

Contents

1

Introduction

Oh motherhood... so beautiful and so brutal

T his book is for all of the soon to be moms or brand new moms out there. Congratulations! You are entering into an entire new era of your life. Arguably, the best and most rewarding era.

There are so many beautiful moments in motherhood. The growth of your child is obvious and expected but the amount of growth that YOU will see in yourself during this journey... that will absolutely throw you for a loop. You don't realize how much you will morph into someone you didn't know you could be. And it truly is a beautiful and better version of yourself.

Now let's get into the nitty gritty stuff...

A harsh truth - mommin' ain't easy. Most days won't feel

rewarding or be overly exciting. The days (and nights) can be SO long. Everyone will have unwarranted opinions or advice about how or why you are doing what you're doing. You will likely question yourself and what to do next every single day, if not every hour. And there will be days where you feel like the most unproductive person ever. Oh, and don't forget the ever-impending and unavoidable mom guilt when you leave the house for one hour by yourself and feel horrible for leaving your baby... ugh.

I don't say all of this to scare you or make you dread parenting. Quite the opposite - I say this to prepare you. Prepare you for the tough moments and to know that YOU ARE NOT ALONE!

Parenting is truly wild and not for the weak. However, people do it every day and you are just as strong as the next mama out there. REMEMBER THAT!

A quick bit about me and my motherhood journey. I have a two-year old son and was fortunate enough to be surrounded with supportive family and kind friends for most of his life so far. I have also been fortunate enough to work from home his entire life allowing me to really watch him develop and be present. However, juggling work life and mom life have been proven to be mentally difficult. Motherhood is draining in general and a nine to five job on top of that...oof.

As a mom you are in your own head A LOT and you don't always have the opportunity to ask for help. You need to learn how to manage these imposing thoughts and crazy incidents on your own. I found that I needed mantras and reminders that helped me in those truly tough moments.

The six lessons and mantras that I selected are ones that I turned to countless times and still internally repeat almost everyday. Whether it's during a long night with a teething baby, during a public toddler meltdown, or a moment of just needing to give myself grace, these lessons and mantras will help bring you back to some semblance of sanity. These got me through and I want to share them with all new moms.

I hope you find these lessons as useful as I do as you are learning and adapting to becoming a mom. Burn these into your brain and bring them forward during your tough days, share them with a fellow mom friend and even your partner.

Let's dive into these lessons and mantras. Perhaps some of it will help you see what to expect during your early motherhood journey.

2

Lesson 1: One person isn't meant to do everything all the time

This was a tough lesson to learn. Whether you're a stay-at-home mom or working mom, the need to "juggle it all" never ceases. Between errands, scheduling appointments, play dates, planning meals, making sure your child is developing, and everything in between; exhaustion and defeat is inevitable.

If you try to do everything for everybody, either your mental health or physical health will deteriorate. So, how do you remedy this?

Partly, it's not giving yourself a hard time when you can't do it all. The other part is delegating and learning how to ask for help. Whether it's your family, friends, neighbors, whoever... find people that will come to your aid when you are feeling overwhelmed.

The other option is to adjust your plans and expectations. If you've had a long day of cleaning and taking care of the baby, and you didn't get the chance to get groceries so now dinner plans are screwed, then make the executive decision to make it a take out night.

It's just really not worth your mental health to worry about something that doesn't need to be a big deal. If you think something is going to push you over the edge, figure out how to pivot and make things easier.

As I mentioned, I had a REALLY hard time coming to grips with this. And I still struggle and have to consciously work at it every single day.

I recall one day where I was huffing and puffing around the house while my husband was home. Our son was crying a lot that day for some unknown reason and just wanted to be held all day long. I had been trying to clean, get work done, make phone calls, get dinner ready... all the things. And as I gave an exasperated sigh as I entered the kitchen with my son on my hip, my husband asked "what's wrong?"

Of course, that sent me into a childish tantrum because I wanted him to just KNOW what was wrong. In reality, he hadn't really seen the cleaning that I was doing because he had been working in the garage most of the day. He didn't know all the unfinished work tasks I had to do for my job because I didn't tell him. Bottom line, I didn't communicate with him that I needed help. I shouldn't have expected him to just know how and why I was feeling overwhelmed.

That's where it becomes important to communicate. Nay, over communicate. Share what you have going on with your partner, so they know just how much is on your plate on a given day. This way they can help you get things done versus you taking it all on.

Whenever I am feeling frustrated or overwhelmed because of how much I have going on, I repeat this to myself "no one was meant to do everything all the time." Nor does anyone expect you to.

After saying that sweet little mantra, it's important to assess and adjust which tasks you need to tackle to make the day more bearable.

napped. That's also VERY PRODUCTIVE.

A lot of motherhood is changing your perspective on things. Napping while your baby naps is productive because then you are more rested and ready to take on the rest of the day with your baby.

Just the other day, I had a checklist that was a mile long and I woke up feeling like I was going to do it all. I got a few things done in the morning and when my son went down for a nap, I thought "alright, let's get the rest of this stuff done!"

Then my husband unexpectedly had the remainder of the afternoon off and he wanted to just snuggle and watch our favorite show together. So, we did and it was so nice to have that alone time together doing something so simple and relaxing. Then my son got up from his nap and I figured I could have my husband watch him while I got things done.

My son was a little cranky and only wanted me. He wanted to watch his show together and play trains with me. So, we did. And guess what, life went on. Nobody was going to be hard on me about not having a productive day besides myself. So, I decided to say "that WAS a productive day." I relaxed, which I desperately needed, and my boys were happy to spend time with me. Absolutely productive.

Bottom line, don't let a to do list dictate what makes you productive when you're a mom. Remember that your child will not remember all of the arbitrary things that you did or didn't do that day. They will remember how they felt being around their mom though. So, as long as you are giving them the love and care they need, that is all the productivity necessary for any given day.

5

Lesson 4: What to do or not do while they are awake or asleep

A good follow up to the previous lesson is how you can be more productive while your child is awake or asleep. I don't remember where I heard this from or who said it but it sure was helpful even though it seems so simple.

It is important to be selective about WHAT you are going to get done around the house by being thoughtful about WHEN you are going to do it. As your child grows there are going to be certain tasks that get harder to do while they are awake.

For example, when your child isn't crawling yet, you are able to easily fold laundry while they lay down next to you. However, that same task becomes increasingly difficult as they start crawling and becoming interested in grabbing things. Don't even get me started about when they start walking and barrel through all of your neatly folded piles.

Some of the tasks that I do while my toddler is asleep are: make important phone calls, fold laundry, clean things that need to be cleaned with chemicals, or do work on my computer.

Those same tasks are SO difficult to accomplish while he is awake because he either wants to scream while I'm talking on the phone, bang on my computer with me, or he just wants my attention.

Things I can do while he is awake are take out the trash, sweep, put laundry in the washer/dryer, unload the dishwasher, etc.

As your child becomes a toddler, the things that you do while they are awake will still take a long time. But it's important for your child to learn how to help with tasks, and to be honest, they WANT to.

My little guy loves to help me load the washer and dryer. It has to be one of his favorite things. He adorably sprints to his clothes hamper and drags it to the laundry room where he proceeds to put clothing items in the washer one by one. He also usually likes to inspect each of them, show me, and talk about the color of the article of clothing.

Seriously, it's the cutest but it also takes FOR-EV-ER. However, he's learning how to be a big helper, he is proud of himself for accomplishing the task, he is learning how to do laundry, and he is spending quality time with me. All of this is SO much more important than moving through the task quickly.

Every kid is different, so perhaps you won't have the same laundry pile destroyer yet laundry loading helper that I do. My point is, learn when it is best for you to get things done so that if you want to have a more productive day, you potentially can by planning accordingly.

6

Lesson 5: Patience, patience, patience

P robably one of the toughest ongoing lessons, especially as you get into toddler hood is maintaining patience. Toddlers were literally made to test the boundaries. They are discovering and learning the world around them and most days it's a beautiful thing... and other days it feels like you're taking crazy pills.

Let's set the scene, shall we. Your toddler woke up at 5:45 AM on the wrong side of the crib (figuratively) and has been whining or crying for three hours. You have been trying to give them everything they want. You finally break down at around 9:00 AM and let them watch their favorite show so you can get some things done. BUT they have other plans for you. They have an absolute screaming fit until you sit down with them to watch the show together. After two hours you tell them that it's time for lunch and screen time is over. They scream. They kick. They scream some more.

You start asking them what they want for lunch. Everything

is a screech begging for screen time. Your head feels like it's going to explode.

You finally make the decision for them and make them a PB&J. Just for them to say NO and that they want cheese. You bring them the cheese and take away the PB&J since they clearly didn't want it. Then they scream bloody murder at you for taking it away. You put the PB&J back. They scream at you for that. You are just about to lose it and yell at them but STOP....

These moments are common, especially for toddlers as they are learning to navigate their emotions and what they are able to get away with. When you are in the midst of these really trying moments, as much as you want to break down and lose your cool, you have to realize that this is when your child needs your patience the most. You've got to dig deeper than you thought you could.

On these kinds of days, clearly there is something going on with your child and even though you can't figure it out, they just need you to be patient and help them through it.

That scenario above is a true story. In fact, that probably happens once a week in my house. It's a very real story for most parents at some point. If you need to, remember that you can always take a minute to collect yourself before responding or trying something different for your child.

No joke, taking a deep breath and saying "Be patient. He/she needs your patience right now more than you need to scream."

Again, it is okay to feel overwhelmed and frustrated by these kinds of experiences. We aren't tin-women with no heart and endless serenity. There will be times where you don't maintain patience. Your screw will bust loose. You might yell directly or indirectly at your child.

After that moment passes, gather yourself. Apologize to your child. Explain to them that you both are having a hard day but you will figure it out together and that you love them. The recovery from those moments is more important than dwelling on what happened in the not so great moment.

Be patient with your child and with yourself. You got this mama.

7

Lesson 6: Trust your instincts

I'm sure you've heard the term "trust your gut." Well, the mom gut is the strongest and most instinctual sign that you have to tell you what to do in any situation with your child.

As a new mom, you will find yourself questioning every little thing between "do they need to wear socks even though it's 85 degrees outside" or "my child never cries this much and I truly think something is wrong."

I don't have any science to back this up but I will go ahead and confidently say that eight out of ten times, you are likely right about whatever decision you are going to make.

For example, one early morning when my son was about nine months old, he started crying, relentlessly. I checked all the things - dirty diaper, he wasn't hungry, he didn't want to be outside, tummy time was a no, and every other little thing that I could think of, I tried it.

He felt a little feverish. For some reason, I started to look up signs of ear infections but he wasn't really showing any of the common symptoms listed. Many of the articles and blogs I read specifically said that ear infections typically don't cause fever. However, some mom groups I was in did say that their child had a fever when they had an ear infection. It was hard to read between the lines and really know.

Although nothing I read was pointing to the possibility that he could have an ear infection, I was convinced. If it wasn't that, I just knew something wasn't right. I took him to urgent care within three hours of the ordeal starting and sure enough, the poor little guy had a double ear infection.

Again, not that you're ALWAYS going to be right but my point is, trust your gut. My husband constantly reminds me to do this when I am rattling off things that I think can be wrong. He encourages me to trust my instincts.

There are also so many instances where your close family is going to tell you what they think might be wrong or what you should do. I have lost count of how many times my parents and in-laws have told me that my child needs a jacket or asked if I have something warmer for my child to wear. I have had to fight giving the biggest eye roll ever so many times and just nicely say, "I've got everything we need, thanks."

Try to figure out nice ways to respond to these kinds of situations. However, also know that if someone is incessant and constantly questioning your choices as a mom, you have every right to (nicely) put them in their place.

Feel free to use this one that I have used a handful of times, "I'm his/her mother and I know what's best for them. I understand you're trying to be helpful but I find it disrespectful that you question my choices so often. Please respect my parental boundaries. No hard feelings. I just need to parent my child my way and will ask for your opinion if I'm ever unsure of something."

Not too harsh but makes a point that you're not going to deal with their antics any longer. A line in the sand has been drawn and they likely will not say another word about your child's missing jacket, socks, etc.

Remember, your baby was literally a part of you. Don't let your loved ones or anyone else make you feel like your instincts aren't right. You know your baby better than anyone and your job is to take care of them to the best of your ability.

8

Conclusion

You are going to do amazing...

Motherhood is the most heart warming while somehow heart wrenching experience. Truly, no one is able to fully prepare you for it. That's another attribute that makes being a mom so special and individualized.

Everyone's parenting journey might have similarities but they are never the same because every person is different. Everyone is unique and your purpose is to figure out every uniqueness about your child and help them work through it, build on it, or grow from it.

Ultimately, you are here to help your child through the journey of life and prepare them to eventually leave you one day. I know, that is super sad to think about BUT it's the truth. We are raising our children to go out into this wild world and not only survive but thrive.

All of the lessons that we went over will help you do that and hopefully you will be a better parent for it. More importantly, it will help your child be the best person that they can be.

A few other reminders...

Listen to everyone's advice and opinions but be selective about what you actually put into action. Again, you know your child best, so what worked for someone else might not work for you... RIGHT NOW... put all advice in a drawer in the back of that beautiful brain of yours in case at one point it becomes useful.

Do not make things a big deal that don't need to be. You will expend so much mental and physical energy constantly, especially in the first few years of motherhood. Don't waste any energy on things that truly don't matter... for example, your kid's clothes getting dirty - they can be changed OR some stranger at a grocery store telling you that your baby should be wearing socks - their opinion doesn't matter.

Be mentally and physically present as much as possible. The cliche is true - time really does fly by. The second you leave the hospital with your newborn, they are practically one year old! But seriously, when you are playing with them, really be there. Interact with them, play pretend, help them develop and have fun. They are always watching or listening to you, even when you think they aren't.

Lastly, be sure to take some time for yourself here and there. This is something I need to desperately work on. Even if it's for an hour or two to go window shopping, get your nails done or go eat a meal by yourself in peace. Having moments to think by yourself without your child needing you is important for your mental health. Except the help when someone offers to babysit and go take some much deserved time to yourself.

I truly hope that these lessons and mantras help you at least once during your motherhood journey. I know they helped me during countless tiresome days.

You are in the midst of one of the greatest gifts that life has to offer, raising a child. Do your best. Be present. Give yourself grace. Take everything in. Help and compliment other moms when you can and enjoy every second of raising your child.

Best of luck mama!

Made in the USA
Las Vegas, NV
31 January 2024

85135212R00017